MW01233157

Essential Question
How do traditions connect people?

Maple Sugar Moon

by Cheryl Minnema
Mille Lacs Band of Ojibwe
Illustrated by Kristina Rodanas

Chapter 1
Waiting

On a cold March day in 1864, Omadwe and her dog Bezhig stood by the woods. Omadwe looked at the snow-covered field. It was as empty as her stomach. The hunters had left three days ago, and there was still no sign of them.

Omadwe followed her **shallow** gray footprints back to the village. Her stomach growled. "Bezhig," she said, "I'm hungry." Bezhig wagged his tail.

It had been a long winter with little meat. In the last **decade**, settlers had taken land that was part of the Fond du Lac reservation. The settlers paid men from the reservation to cut down trees. Many men had been hurt cutting down trees. One had even died.

There were now only five hunters left in the village. Omadwe's father, Young Kegg, was one of them.

Omadwe had watched her father get ready for the trip. He put his new hatchet in his belt. Young Kegg had **traded** with the settlers for the hatchet.

"The settlers are changing the ways of our **ancestors**," said Omadwe. "They took our land. Now they want us to be like them."

Her father hugged Omadwe. "We are the People. We will not let them change us."

STOP AND CHECK

What has the winter been like for Omadwe's village?

4

Chapter 2
Best Friends

Omadwe rubbed her stomach. The pain wasn't just from hunger. She was afraid her father would not come back. The **intensity** of her fear made her stomach hurt.

Zhaawan's father hadn't come back. He had been killed while cutting down trees.

Zhaawan had been Omadwe's best friend, But last fall, Zhaawan wanted to be called "Angelina." In October, her family moved from their wigwam to a wooden house. Then Zhaawan began criticizing and making fun of Omadwe's clothes.

"Why do you wear those dirty leather scraps?" Zhaawan would ask as she **admired** her own blue cotton dress. "Your father could trade furs for a dress like mine."

Omadwe had ignored her. But Omadwe missed her friend who had become Angelina.

After her father had died, Zhaawaan and her mother had moved in with her father's family. Zhaawan rarely left her grandma's wigwam. This surprised Omadwe. She thought that Zhaawan loved her wooden house.

Suddenly, Bezhig bolted after a waabooz (rabbit). "Bezhig! Wait!" called Omadwe. Bezhig did not have the speed or **endurance** to catch the waabooz. He'd soon **forfeit** the chase and return.

Then Omadwe heard the cawing of an aandeg (crow). Hearing the aandeg was an **honor**. It was the first sign of maple sugaring season!

Chapter 3
The Sound of the Aandeg

Omadwe ran home with Bezhig to share the news. She heard noise in the village. Had they already heard the aandeg?

Then Omadwe saw her father. He had a deer and the other hunters had rabbits. The men had returned safely! She thanked the Great Spirit as she ran to Young Kegg.

Omadwe hugged her father. Then she remembered the crows. "I heard the aandeg!" she shouted.

A few days later, Omadwe was in her wigwam rolling up cattail mats. Her mother, Ikwe, handed her some pouches.

"Put these outside with the food supply," Ikwe said.

Omadwe opened the flap of the wigwam and saw four new pairs of snowshoes on the ground outside. She smiled back at her mother.

"We're going to the maple sugar camp today," said Ikwe.

"But why four pairs?" asked Omadwe.

"Zhaawan will be joining us this year," replied her mother.

Omadwe put the **pouches** by the food supply. She was glad that Zhaawan would be coming with them.

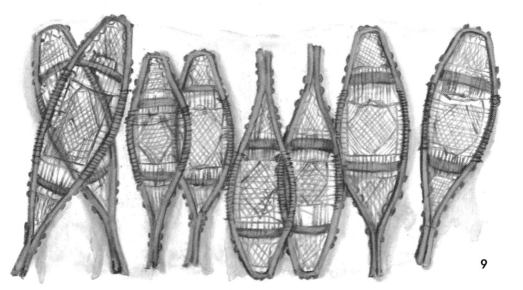

Later, as Omadwe walked with her parents through the village, she wondered how Zhaawan would be.

At the edge of the village, Omadewe saw Zhaawan peek out of her grandma's wigwam. Then she slowly stepped out. She wore her old buckskin dress.

"Aaniin (Hi), Angelina," said Omadwe.

Zhaawan took a deep breath. "Please don't call me Angelina. I'm sorry for being mean to you," she said.

"You're my friend, always," Omadwe said and hugged her. Then she helped Zhaawan lace up her snowshoes.

STOP AND CHECK

How has Zhaawan changed since her father died?

Chapter 4
Maple Sugar Camp

They reached the maple sugar camp after a day of travel. Young Kegg used his hatchet to make cuts in the maples. Then he put wooden spouts in the trees while Ikwe set up their camp.

Once the taps were in place, Omadwe and Zhaawan put birch bark baskets under each spout. The girls couldn't wait for the baskets to fill up. They each lay underneath a spout with their mouths open.

"Mmmm," said Omadwe.

But before Zhaawan could get a taste, Bezhig began licking her face. Zhaawan **despised** it when the dog licked her face. "Gego (Don't)! You're so **irritating**!" she said. Omadwe laughed.

As darkness fell, Young Kegg made a fire. After a dinner of wild rice and deer meat, Omadwe and Zhaawan settled into the wigwam and fell asleep.

In the morning, Zhaawan gave Omadwe
a necklace of shiny red beads. "I traded
my blue dress for it," said Zhaawan.

"But you loved that dress," replied Omadwe.

Zhaawan hugged her. "I don't want anything
that reminds me of the settlers. Please take the
necklace," she said.

All morning, Omadwe and Zhaawan **gathered**
firewood and emptied maple water from the
birch bark baskets. Then it was time to boil the
water into syrup.

Young Kegg poured the water into the kettle,
and Ikwe stirred it with a wooden paddle. Each
time it was about to boil over, Omadwe stirred it
with a pine branch. The bubbling foam **retreated**
as soon as the pine branch touched it.

That evening, the girls had hard maple candy with their dinner.

"Look," Zhaawan said, pointing up at the full moon. "It's a maple sugar moon!" Omadwe laughed, happy that Zhaawan was here to share her joy during maple sugar time.

STOP AND CHECK

How do Omadwe and her family make maple syrup?

Summarize

Summarize the main events in *Maple Sugar Moon*. Your graphic organizer may help.

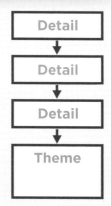

Text Evidence

1. How does Omadwe's father make her feel better about the settlers? THEME

2. Find the word *criticizing* on page 5. What does it mean? What clues on page 6 helped you figure it out? VOCABULARY

3. Write about why Omadwe is excited to hear the crows and what maple sugar camp means to her. Use details from the text in your answer.
   WRITE ABOUT READING

Compare Texts

Read about the real-life inspiration for Omadwe and her story.

Maple Sugar

The story *Maple Sugar Moon* was inspired by my Ojibwe grandmother, Lucy Kegg Clark. Her Ojibwe name was Omadwebigaashiikwe (the sound of waves coming onto the shore). She was called Omadwe for short. Her parents were named Young Kegg and Chi ikwe zan(s).

A metal spout and bucket are used to collect sap from a maple tree.

Omadwe told many stories of harvesting maple sugar at a camp in Minnesota. She went with her parents and other family members. There was always a dog popping up somewhere in these stories.

17

This photograph was taken in 1908. It shows a Native American woman with birch bark baskets used for collecting sap.

In *Maple Sugar Moon*, the dog's name is Bezhig, which means "one."

Omadwe was hesitant about modern-day inventions. She would often try a new way of doing things. But then she would quickly return to the old way.

Omadwe's family harvested sap from maple trees in the spring. A tap or spout was put in the tree to drain the sap. Birch bark baskets were used to collect it. The sap was then boiled for hours until it turned into a thick syrup. Eventually it turned into sugar. It took 40 gallons of sap to make just one gallon of maple syrup!

Make Connections

Why do you think the author wanted to write about her grandmother? ESSENTIAL QUESTION

How does "Maple Sugar" help you understand more about the maple sugar camp in *Maple Sugar Moon*? TEXT TO TEXT

Focus on Genre

Historical Fiction Historical fiction tells a made-up story that is set in the past. It often gives information about a real event. Sometimes it is about real people who were living at the time. Historical fiction helps us understand life long ago.

Read and Find *Maple Sugar Moon* is not a true story, but it is based on real events in the life of the author's grandmother. Find one detail in the story that is based on fact. Then find one detail that is probably made up. Explain your answer.

Your Turn

Native Americans have a tradition of telling stories aloud. The stories tell about the past and keep their culture alive. Think of a person or an event in your family that you could tell a story about. You can make up some details to add interest, but base your story on facts. Practice telling your story aloud. Then share it with others.